LIBRARY
LONGFELLOW ELEMENTARY

THE LEOPARD

THE BIG CAT DISCOVERY LIBRARY

Lynn M. Stone

Rourke Enterprises, Inc.
Vero Beach, Florida 32964

© 1989 Rourke Enterprises, Inc.

All rights reserved. No part of this book may be reproduced or utilized in any form or by any means, electronic or mechanical including photocopying, recording or by any information storage and retrieval system without permission in writing from the publisher.

PHOTO CREDITS
© Lynn M. Stone: Pages 7, 8, 10, 18, 21; © Leonard Lee Rue III/DRK Photo: Page 1; © Peter Pickford/DRK Photo: Page 4; © Jeff Foott/DRK Photo: Cover; © Terry G. Murphy/Animals Animals: Pages 12-13; © Michael Dick/Animals Animals: Page 15; © Ahup and Manoj Shah/ Animals Animals: Page 17

ACKNOWLEDGEMENTS

The author wishes to thank the following for special photographic assistance in the preparation of this book: Catherine Hilker and the Cincinnati Zoo; Nancy Tetzlaf and Jungle Larry's Safari, Naples, Fla.

Library of Congress Cataloging-in-Publication Date
Stone, Lynn M.
    Leopards / Lynn M. Stone.
      p. cm. — (The big cat discovery library)
    Includes index.
    Summary: An introduction to the physical characteristics, habits, natural environment, relationship to humans, and future of the spotted leopard, the most adaptable of the big cats.
    ISBN 0-86592-502-X
    1. Leopards—Juvenile literature [1. Leopards.] I. Title. II. Series: Stone, Lynn M. Big cat discovery library.
QL737.C23S769 1989   89-32642
599.74'428—dc20   CIP
                                  AC

TABLE OF CONTENTS

The Leopard	5
The Leopard's Cousins	6
How They look	9
Where The Live	11
How They Live	14
The Leopard's Cubs	16
Predator and Prey	19
Leopards and People	20
The Leopard's Future	22
Glossary	23
Index	24

THE LEOPARD

The life of the graceful leopard *(Panthera pardus)* might well be marked "Top Secret". Leopards are big, spotted cats about which someone said, "They're everywhere and nowhere at once."

Leopards aren't really everywhere, although a fair number live in many parts of Asia and Africa. But leopards are very difficult to see. Except in wildlife **preserves**, leopards live secret lives, usually staying out of people's sight.

Leopards have done better than other big cats in surviving changes to their home, or **habitat**. The leopard can sometimes adjust its ways enough to survive the changes that man makes. This ability makes them the most **adaptable** of the big cats.

African Leopard with Impala

THE LEOPARD'S COUSINS

The leopard is a member of the cat, or **feline**, family. Despite its much greater size, the leopard is related to the house cat. The leopard's closest cousin is the jaguar, the big, spotted cat of South America.

Tigers and lions are close relatives, too. Tigers, lions, leopards, and jaguars are the "roaring" cats. None of the other cats has a voice box quite like these four.

The rare snow leopard *(Panthera uncia)* of central Asia is an altogether different animal than the spotted leopard. The thick-furred snow leopard has leopard spots, but it does not roar. The snow leopard is a cat of cold, rocky mountains.

Snow Leopard

HOW THEY LOOK

Leopards are strikingly beautiful cats. Most leopards have both solid black spots and doughnut-like spots on their yellowish fur. The color of a leopard and the size of its spots changes somewhat with each group of leopards. Judean Desert leopards, for example, are much lighter than most other leopards.

Leopards can also be nearly pure black. Often called "black panthers", black leopards and spotted leopards can be born in the same **litter**.

The biggest leopards are about nine feet long and weigh up to 170 pounds. Most leopards weigh about 100 pounds.

The leopard's coat helps **camouflage**, or hide, it. Black fur blends into the dark forests where black leopards are generally found.

Black Asian Leopard

WHERE THEY LIVE

Leopards are found in nearly all of Africa and in much of Asia. Leopards live in such widely separated places as India, Iran, Java, China, Russia, Arabia, Nepal, Israel, Kenya, and South Africa.

Leopards can live in forests, grasslands, swampy areas, and dry, desert-like regions. On Africa's Mt. Kenya, they have been found at 15,000 feet above sea level!

Many leopards live in dripping forests where the rain falls day after day. Others live in areas so dry that their only source of water is in what they eat.

African Leopard

African Leopard

HOW THEY LIVE

Leopards may be active at any time of day, except where they have learned to fear people. Then they become animals of the night.

Leopards are fine climbers and leapers. On branches they stretch out with their legs hanging on both sides like giant rag dolls.

Like house cats, leopards dislike stepping in water, but they swim easily when they have to.

Leopards travel alone. They move quietly and very carefully. Their keen eyes and ears help them avoid danger. Leopards are so careful and adaptable that they have learned to live in areas where people have built homes and farms.

Like other big cats, leopards spend much of their time hunting or resting.

African Leopard

THE LEOPARD'S CUBS

A mother leopard usually bears two or three cubs. They are born blind in a cave, hollow, or some other well-hidden place. The cubs open their eyes when they are about 10 days old.

The mother leopard rears her babies. Only rarely does a male leopard help.

At three months of age, the cubs begin to follow their mother on hunts. A few weeks later they begin killing small animals. They stay with the mother, however, for 18 months to two years before going off on their own.

Leopards in zoos have lived 23 years.

Black Asian Leopard

PREDATOR AND PREY

Leopards are **predators**, or hunters. A leopard feeds on other animals, its **prey**.

The sharp-eyed leopard usually hunts by **stalking**, moving carefully and slowly toward prey. The leopard finally bounds from hiding and lunges for its victim's throat.

Leopards eat wildebeest, zebras, small antelope, birds, snakes, baboons, sheep, and almost anything else. They also feed on the kills of other predators.

Leopards are extremely strong. African leopards often drag a heavy animal up into a tree. There it is safe from lions, vultures, and hyenas.

Leopards themselves are sometimes killed by lions, tigers, or wild dogs.

Leopard Prey: Wildebeest

LEOPARDS AND PEOPLE

Like all big cats, leopards have held the interest of people for hundreds of years. Early people told tales about how the leopard got its spots.

Another tale explained how the leopard became such a great hunter. The leopard, said the ancient Greeks, had sweet breath. The sweetness drew animals to the leopard. Then the sweetness overcame them, making them helpless in front of the big cat.

Except in zoos, circuses, and African wildlife preserves, people rarely see leopards. Still, leopards are feared. Man-eating leopards are unusual. One Indian leopard, however, reportedly killed over 200 people in the 1850s.

African Leopard in Zoo

THE LEOPARD'S FUTURE

In the 1960s and 1970s thousands of leopards were poisoned or shot for their fur. Most countries no longer permit the sale of leopard skins. Several African countries, however, raise large numbers of farm animals and have been killing leopards. Farmers in these nations fear leopard attacks on their animals.

Leopards often feed on remains of animals that they didn't kill. Farmers put poison on the dead animals. The leopards eat the poisoned meat.

As the human population grows, the leopard's natural habitat shrinks. The leopard is adaptable, however. Because of that, there will probably always be leopards living on the free side of bars and fences.

Glossary

adaptable (a DAPT a bull)—an animal's ability to change its habits to match a changing habitat

camouflage (KEM o flahj)—to hide by matching an animal's colors to its surroundings

feline (FEE line)—any of the cats

habitat (HAB a tat)—the area in which an animal lives

litter (LIT er)—group of baby animals born of the same mother at the same time

predator (PRED a tor)—an animal that kills other animals for food

preserve (pre ZERV)—an area where wild animals are protected from man

prey (PRAY)—an animal that is hunted for food by another animal

stalking (STAWK ing)—hunting by moving slowly and quietly toward prey

INDEX

age	16	length	9
cats	5, 6	man-eater	20
claws	6	panther, black	9
color	9	people	20
cubs	16	prey	16, 19
food	16, 19	range	11
fur	9, 22	senses	14
habitat	5, 11, 22	size	9
hunting	19, 22	voice	6
jaguar	6	weight	9

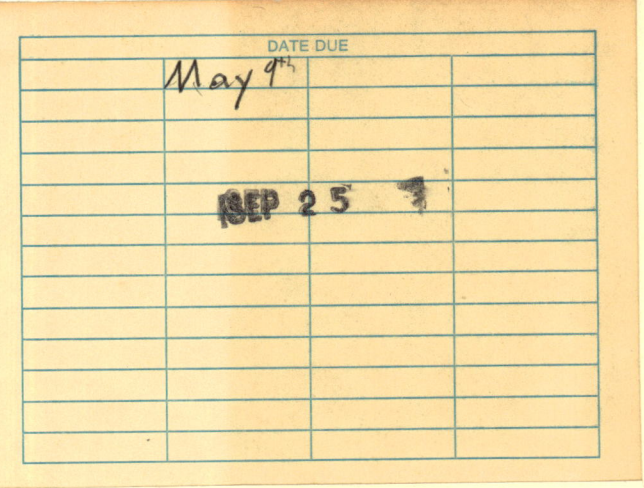

599.7   Stone, Lynn M.   **10287**
STO
             The leopard.

**LONGFELLOW ELEM SCHOOL
HOUSTON TX 77025**

415080 01026 58772A 08882E   017